THIS IS MY BRAIN!

A BOOK ON NEURODIVERSITY

ELISE GRAVEL

CHRONICLE BOOKS
SAN FRANCISCO

Library of Congress Cataloging-in-Publication Data:

Names: Gravel, Elise, author, illustrator.
Title: This is my brain! : a book on neurodiversity / Elise Gravel.
Description: San Francisco : Chronicle Books, [2024] | Audience: Ages 8–12.
| Summary: "In this seriously funny book, acclaimed creator Elise Gravel
uses her trademark humor and punchy art to celebrate the many
wonderful ways humans think and to show readers that understanding how
different brains feel and learn can help us connect with others . . .
and keep our own brains happy!"—Provided by publisher.
Identifiers: LCCN 2023058917 | ISBN 9781797228204 (hardcover)
Subjects: LCSH: Brain—Comic books, strips, etc. | Brain—Juvenile
literature. | Neurodiversity—Comic books, strips, etc. |
Neurodiversity—Juvenile literature.
Classification: LCC QP376 .G693 2024 | DDC 612.82—dc23/eng/20231221
LC record available at https://lccn.loc.gov/2023058917

Manufactured in China.

Design by Elise Gravel and Sara Gillingham Studio.
Font designed by Elise Gravel.

10 9 8 7 6 5 4 3 2

Chronicle Books LLC
680 Second Street
San Francisco, California 94107

Chronicle Books—we see things differently.
Become part of our community at www.chroniclekids.com.

To every child and grown-up child
who feels "different":
Your brain is beautiful. —E. G.

EACH OF US HAS A

Brains don't look like much,
but they have many

SUPERPOWERS!

Our brain controls
everything our body does.
It's our brain that . . .

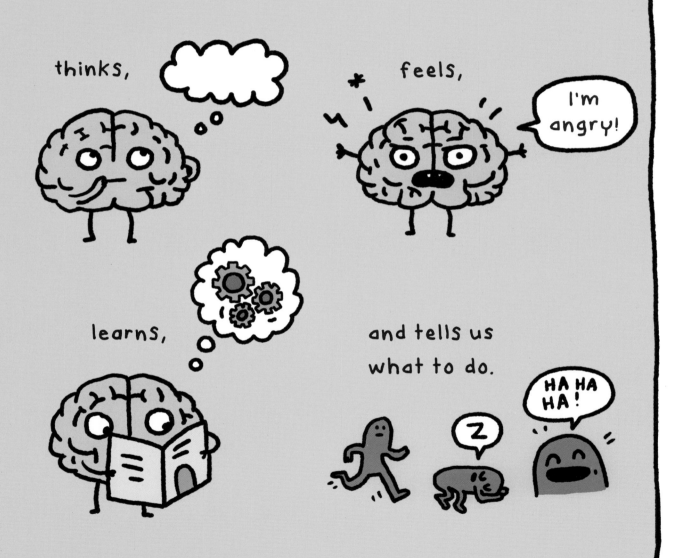

Our **SENSES**

collect information
from the world around us—

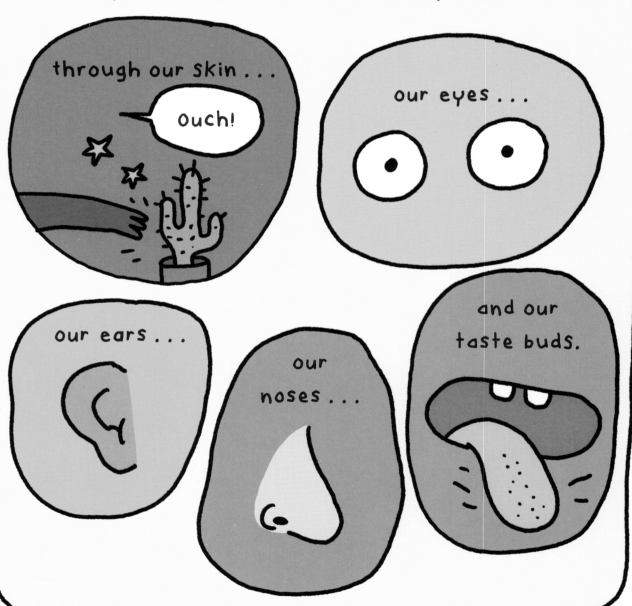

through our skin . . .

Ouch!

our eyes . . .

our ears . . .

our noses . . .

and our taste buds.

Our brain receives the information sent by our senses.

 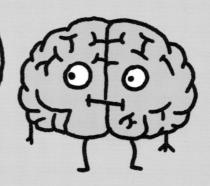

It processes that information . . .

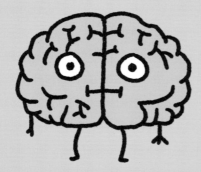 

and sends a message back to our body.

Do you know who have
the BUSIEST brains?

BABIES AND KIDS!

When we are babies, we are little

LEARNING MACHINES.

Think about it: When we're born, we don't know **ANYTHING** except how to

And we keep learning new things our **ENTIRE** lives.

Grandpa, what was the biggest dinosaur?

I don't know! Let's look it up in this book!

And each brain learns in a

DIFFERENT WAY.

I learn better when I can touch things.

I learn better when my teacher is funny!

I learn better when I'm alone.

I learn better when I'm with a friend.

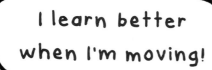

I learn better when I'm moving!

I learn better when I play!

Some people learn better when they get some **HELP.** Others prefer to learn **BY THEMSELVES.**

Some people learn by
asking a lot of questions.

Why do dogs
wag their tails?

Why do we Sneeze?

How do bees
make honey?

Some prefer to
observe quietly.

And some need
to use their hands
and experiment.

EVERYTHING WE DO and EVERYTHING that happens around us can help us LEARN.

We learn when we have FUN.

We learn when we WATCH others.

We learn when we make mistakes.

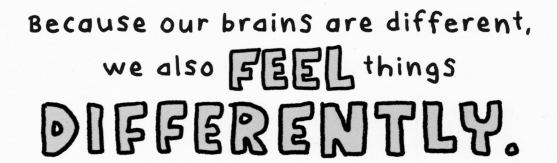

Because our brains are different, we also **FEEL** things **DIFFERENTLY.**

There are no good ways
or bad ways to feel things.

ALL OUR FEELINGS
ARE VALID

and can teach us something.

We all see the world in
DIFFERENT WAYS.

It's a bit like our brains are wearing different colored glasses.

Sometimes it can be difficult or confusing to be around people who think, feel, or act **DIFFERENTLY** than we do.

Why won't klev talk to me? Doesn't he like me?

klev doesn't speak like you and I. He communicates in different ways.

Look! He made a drawing for you!

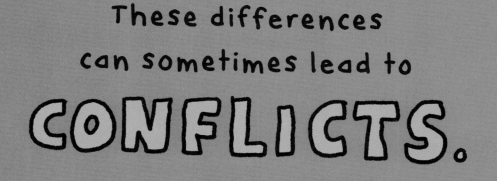

After all, the world would be very **BORING** if our brains were all the same, like something made in a factory.

Thanks to our differences,
we can put our ideas
together . . . and create
BIGGER, BETTER ideas.

Our brains NEVER stop learning.
They are like muscles, and
we can help them **GROW**
and stay strong!

Here's how:

Read books.

Try new things.

I baked a cake all by myself!

Move your body.

Ask questions.

How do phones work?

Eat nutritious foods.

Get enough sleep.

Wear a helmet to protect your brain.

Learn to relax.

Sometimes our brains face challenges and struggles, just like our bodies do. When this happens, we can help our brains by

TALKING TO SOMEONE.

Telling someone else about our feelings can help our brains

FEEL BETTER.

A TEACHER

A PARENT

A FRIEND

A DOCTOR OR A THERAPIST

Our brains work hard for us!
Let's try to keep them healthy
and HAPPY!

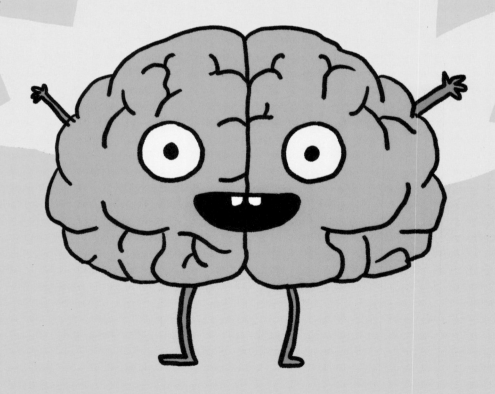